The Smallest
Dinosaurs

The Smallest Dinosaurs

BY SEYMOUR SIMON
ILLUSTRATED BY ANTHONY RAO

Crown Publishers, Inc.
New York

Also by Seymour Simon

The Long View into Space
Animal Fact/Animal Fable
The Long Journey from Space
Your First Home Computer

Library of Congress Cataloging-in-Publication Data

Simon, Seymour
  The smallest dinosaurs.

  Summary: Discusses seven dinosaurs, all about the size of a dog or
chicken, which are believed to be the bird's prehistoric cousin.
    1. Dinosaurs—Juvenile literature.   [1. Dinosaurs]
I. Rao, Anthony.   II. Title.
QE862.D5S53   1982   567.9'1   81-3247
ISBN 0-517-54425-3   AACR2
ISBN 0-517-56550-1 (pbk.)
10 9 8 7 6 5 4

CONTENTS

INTRODUCTION

Long before people
lived on the Earth
dinosaurs lived here.
Dinosaurs are gone now,
but dinosaur bones remain.
These bones are called "fossils."

Scientists have learned
what dinosaurs were like
from their fossils.
They know that some dinosaurs
walked on all four feet.
Others walked
on their hind legs.

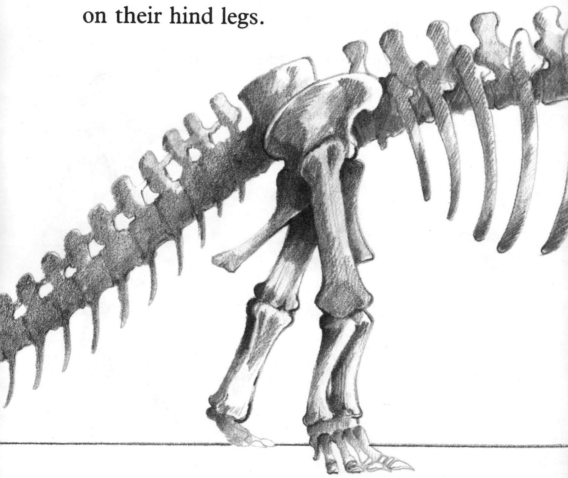

Some dinosaurs were as tall
as a telephone pole,
others were longer than a big bus.
Not all dinosaurs were big.
Some were about your size.
Others were the size
of a dog.
And still others
were no bigger
than a chicken.

Scientists cannot learn
everything from fossils.
They do not know what color
a dinosaur's skin was,
and they are not sure
of other facts as well.
Some scientists think
all dinosaurs were
cold-blooded—
that their
bodies became cool
during cold weather
and warm during
warm weather.

Other scientists believe
small dinosaurs
were warm-blooded—
that their bodies
stayed the same temperature
no matter what the weather was.

11

All of the small dinosaurs
belong to a family named
Coelurosauria
(SEE-lo-SAW-rea),
which means
hollow lizard.
They were given that name
because their bones were
light and hollow.

This book tells about
many small dinosaurs.
It tells how their
small size and
speedy movements
helped them survive
for millions of years.

SALTOPUS
(SAL-tuh-pus)

Saltopus was a
very small dinosaur.
Its name means
leaping foot.
It had a long neck,
like a duck,
a pointy head,
and large eyes.
It weighed
about two pounds.

It was as big
as a cat.
Saltopus was as quick
as a cat, too.
It ran on its
strong hind legs.

It ate small lizards
and other animals.
Its small front legs
looked like arms with hands.
The hands had five fingers.
Saltopus used its fingers
to hold onto the animals
it caught.

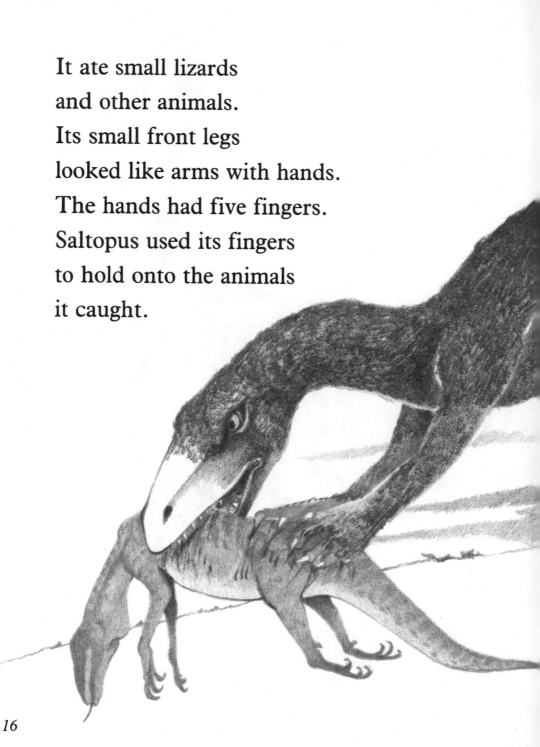

It bit and killed
the animals with
its sharp teeth
and then tore
them to pieces.

COMPSOGNATHUS
(COMP-so-NAY-thus)

One of the smallest dinosaurs
was Compsognathus.
Its name means
fancy jawed.

Compsognathus was about
the size of a pigeon.
This dinosaur
was like a bird
in other ways as well.
Parts of its body
were covered
with feathers.

The feathers helped
Compsognathus keep
its body temperature
the same at all times.
If the air got too cold,
its feathers would fluff up.
This trapped
Compsognathus's body heat
and kept it warm.
If the air got too warm,
its feathers opened.
This let out body heat
and kept Compsognathus cool.

COELOPHYSIS
(SEE-lo-fise-iss)

Coelophysis was another
small dinosaur.
Its name means
hollow boned.
Coelophysis was about
three feet tall.
It had three large
fingers on each hand.
It looked like
Saltopus,
only larger.
Coelophysis weighed
as much as a
medium-sized dog.

Hundreds of Coelophysis bones
were found near
Abiquiu, New Mexico.
This is the only place
in the world
where so many
small dinosaur bones
were found together.
The bones came from
a flock of small dinosaurs.

The small dinosaurs
were trapped in
quicksand
or mud.
No one knows why
the dinosaurs
did not escape.
Perhaps they kept eating
even though they were
sinking into the mud.

STRUTHIOMIMUS
(*STROOTH-ee-o-MY-mus*)

Struthiomimus was
one of the fastest
land animals
that ever lived.
This dinosaur
was about as large
as a grown person.
Its name means
like an ostrich.

Struthiomimus had
a small head
and large eyes.
It could see very well
and could run very fast.

It was good at catching
other animals to eat.
And it could have eaten
fruits and vegetables,
just as ostriches do today.
Struthiomimus had no teeth.

It had a beak
like that of a bird.
Its brain was larger
than the brain of any
bird living today.
Scientists do not know
if it was like a bird
in other ways.
They do not know
if it took care
of its young
like a bird.
They do not know
if it made noises
or if it had a birdlike song.
And they do not know
if it stayed in flocks
as some birds do today.

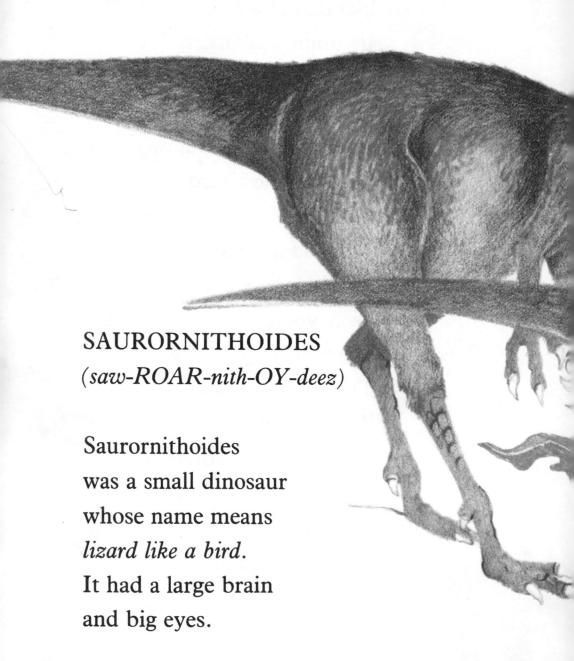

SAURORNITHOIDES
(saw-ROAR-nith-OY-deez)

Saurornithoides
was a small dinosaur
whose name means
lizard like a bird.
It had a large brain
and big eyes.

Its eyes were so big
that some scientists
believe it could see well
in the dark.
It may have hunted
for its food at night.
Perhaps Saurornithoides
was good at catching
the small animals
that came out
to eat plants
after sunset.

DROMAEOSAURUS
(DROM-ee-o-SAW-rus)

Dromaeosaurus was another
birdlike dinosaur.
Its name means
emu-lizard.
An emu looks like
an ostrich
but has shorter legs.
Dromaeosaurus was
about the size
of a grown person.

It was a great hunter.
Its hind legs
were large and strong.
Each foot had
a sharp inner toe.
This toe could spring
out like a knife.
Dromaeosaurus
was also a fast runner.
It would run
after a smaller animal
and grab it
with its long fingers.
Then it would stand
on one hind leg

and kick the animal to pieces
with its sharp toe.
There are few animals today
that could escape
from this great hunter.

ARCHAEOPTERYX
(ARK-ee-OP-ter-icks)

Archaeopteryx
was the strangest
of all the small dinosaurs.
Its name means
old wing.
Fossils show
that Archaeopteryx
had feathers covering
most of its body and arms.
Its arms looked like wings
with claws at the ends.

At one time
scientists thought
Archaeopteryx was a bird.
Then some scientists looked
more closely
at other fossils.
They saw that the
fossil bones
of Archaeopteryx
were almost the same
as the fossil bones of
Compsognathus.

This discovery made them believe
that Archaeopteryx was
a small dinosaur.
Like other small dinosaurs,
Archaeopteryx was
a fast runner.

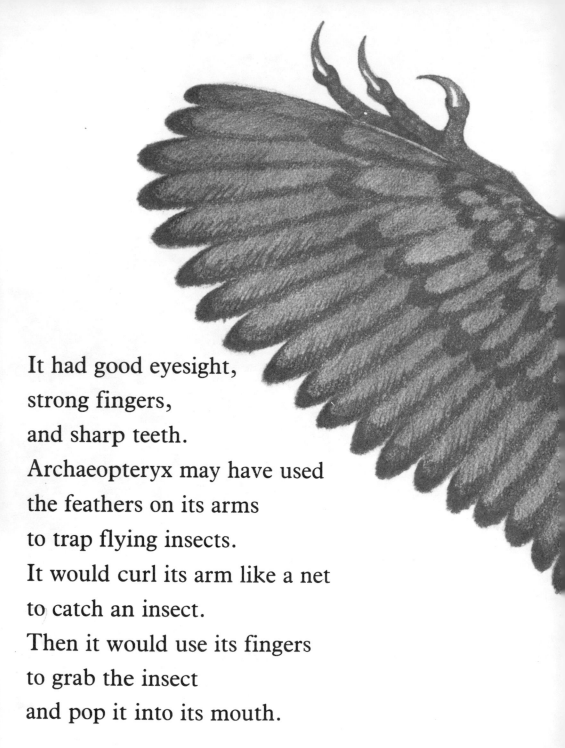

It had good eyesight,
strong fingers,
and sharp teeth.
Archaeopteryx may have used
the feathers on its arms
to trap flying insects.
It would curl its arm like a net
to catch an insect.
Then it would use its fingers
to grab the insect
and pop it into its mouth.

Archaeopteryx could not fly.
But it may have flapped
its wings like a chicken
when it jumped into the air
to catch insects.

It also used the feathers
on its wings and tail
like a brake to make
sudden turns and stops.
The wings helped
Archaeopteryx
to catch its food
and to escape
from larger dinosaurs.
It was warm-blooded
like a bird.
It had a brain
the size of a bird's.
Scientists say
that this small dinosaur
was on its way
to becoming a bird.

LOOKING BACK

Millions of years passed,
and the dinosaurs died.
Other animals appeared.

They changed
as the earth changed.
The next time you see a bird,
think back to the distant past.
You may be looking
at a present-day cousin
of the smallest dinosaurs.